Artic Skits: /r/

A collection of skits for developing speech, language and reading

Kathryn Ross and Kimberly Pruitt

Illustrations by David Utley

www.slpstorytellers.com, Denton, TX

Problem Skill Area:	Articulation, Language, Reading
Developmental Age:	8-13 years
Grade Level:	3rd thru 7th grades

Artic Skits
Skits for /r/ Production Generalization

Written by Kathryn Ross, CCC/SLP
And Kimberly Pruitt
Illustrated by David Utley

All Rights Reserved
No part of this book may be reproduced in any form or means without written permission of www.slpstorytellers.com except for educational purposes by the purchaser of the book and CD.

Inquiries should be addressed to:
www.slpstorytellers.com
First Edition

ISBN-13: 978-0-9725803-9-7
ISBN-10: 0-9725803-9-5

Library of Congress Catalog Card Number: 2005938660

Ross, Kathryn.
    Artic skits— /r/ : a collection of skits for developing speech, language and reading / Kathryn Ross and Kimberly Pruitt ; illustrated by David Utley.
    1st ed.
    92 p. : ill. ; 28 cm. + 1 CD-ROM.
    Workbook and compact disc and pictures, designed to motivate reluctant speech students and readers by using interactive drama. Incorporates techniques that can be adapted for use with speech and language-impaired children. Includes tips for therapists, and for each skit a list of new vocabulary, comprehension questions and answers, language extensions, an activity, and a word list indicating word placement within the text.
    Intended audience: Teachers of children ages 3 and up, in groups of three to six.
    Contents: The little red rooster – Brewster Ryans cracks the case – Rhonda's surprise party – The incredible shrinking twins – Rachel runs the race – The contest.
    ISBN: 9780972580397 (softcover : alk. paper)
    (10-digit): 0972580395 (softcover : alk. paper)

1. Children's plays. 2. Speech—Study and teaching. 3.Language arts—Juvenile drama. 4. Reading (Preschool) I. Pruitt, Kimberly. II. Utley, David, ill. III. Title. IV. Title: Artic skits— r

    [E] 22
    CIP: TxGeoBT   2005938660

Although information herein is based on the author's extensive experience and knowledge, it is not intended to substitute for the services of qualified professionals.

About the Authors

Kathryn Ross, MS, CCC-SLP, is a speech-language pathologist working in the public schools and outpatient rehab settings of Copperas Cove, Texas. She began her career as an educational sign language interpreter before returning to school at Abilene Christian University to become a speech-language pathologist. She and her husband, DeWayne, have been married for fourteen years and have three, soon to be four, beautiful boys.

Kimberly Pruitt is a stay-at-home mom of two beautiful children, Maggie and Phoenix. She and her husband, Mark, work as house parents for developmentally delayed adults in Abilene, Texas. She studied English at Abilene Christian University.

About the Illustrator

David Utley, MFA, is a designer/illustrator who recently finished his masters program at the University of Texas. He received his Bachelor of Arts in Theater from Abilene Christian University. He is honored to illustrate *Artic Skits* for his sister, Kathryn.

Dedication

Artic Skits is dedicated to the students at J.L. Williams Elementary School and Lovett Ledger Intermediate School in Copperas Cove, Texas. Without them, there would have been no inspiration. We would also like to dedicate this book to our families, whose amateur editing gives new meaning to the phrase constructive criticism. We couldn't have done it without you.

Acknowledgment

I wish to thank Wynell LeCroy, Karen Brown, and Lavelle Carlson for applying their various areas of expertise to reading and commenting on *Artic Skits*.

Table of Contents

Introduction 1

Tips for Therapists… 2

The Little Red Rooster… 3
    Skit… 4
    New Vocabulary and Comprehension Questions…............... 8
    Teacher's Guide 9
    Activity 10
    Word List… 11

Brewster Ryans Cracks the Case… 13
    Skit… 14
    New Vocabulary and Comprehension Questions…............. 22
    Teacher's Guide 23
    Activity 25
    Word List… 26

Rhonda's Surprise Party… 27
    Skit… 28
    New Vocabulary and Comprehension Questions…............. 37
    Teacher's Guide 38
    Activity 39
    Word List… 40

The Incredible Shrinking Twins… 41
    Skit… 42
    New Vocabulary and Comprehension Questions…............. 54
    Teacher's Guide 55
    Activity 56
    Word List… 57

Rachel Runs the Race… 59
    Skit… 60
    New Vocabulary and Comprehension Questions…............. 69
    Teacher's Guide 70
    Activity 71
    Word List… 72

The Contest… 73
    Skit… 74
    New Vocabulary and Comprehension Questions…............. 84
    Teacher's Guide 85
    Activity 86
    Activity 87
    Word List… 88

Introduction

Artic Skits fits the needs of speech-language pathologists looking for a fun, efficient, interactive approach to working on articulation at the conversational level, as well as reading, language, and grammar. *Artic Skits* are designed to motivate reluctant speech students and readers by using interactive drama. This book encompasses a wide range of techniques that can be adapted for use with a variety of speech and language impaired children.

Drama is effective because it is multisensory; kinesthetic, visual, and oral. It can be used in a variety of ways. The use of multiple senses facilitates learning and memory. Drama can be used as a way of practicing correct speech and language in a natural setting, and for role-playing real-life situations. The students will hear what they, and others, read and react physically and emotionally to the scripted readings. Drama can help to provide a safe and accepting environment in which students can gain the confidence to experiment and explore language in ways they may otherwise have avoided.

The skits included are intended for use with students in grades 3 and up. Following each skit, you will find various activities that can be used to work on comprehension, vocabulary development, and syntax. The skits are designed to be used with groups of 3 to 6 students, and are effective tools to work on a variety of speech and language areas.

For students working on articulation, targeted speech sounds can be extracted from age-appropriate readings. The students can then listen for and hear the sounds multiple times, allowing them to produce the sounds in a structured, yet naturalistic, context.

While the students are learning correct speech, they will also be learning literacy and language. For struggling readers, the dialogue in the reading passages is short enough that the students will not become fatigued. Reading comprehension and fluency will improve as they add voice, inflection, and body movement to the readings. The scripted dialogue can serve as a good model for appropriate sentence structure and oral grammar. Drama is a great way to illustrate pragmatic language skills including initiating conversation, turn-taking, and non-verbal language.

Often, students have language goals as well as articulation goals. For the teachers of these students, there is a list of suggested language extension activities at the end of each reading. Comprehension questions are also included and these may be tailored to the skill level of each student. The questions are a guide for the speech-language pathologist or teacher. When using them, always keep in mind that the questions alone can be perceived by the student as a test. If necessary, provide scaffolding questions to make it an effective learning experience.

Drama and cartoons are both effective motivators for reluctant readers. These fun and engaging scripts will facilitate conversation with the overall aim of enabling and encouraging the development of speech, language, and communication skills in each individual student.

Tips for Therapists

- At the end of each script, you will find a list of vocabulary words that may be new to your students. Before you introduce the script, review these words and discuss any words that are unfamiliar.

- When you introduce the script, give each student a copy and have him or her highlight the part you would like him or her to read. Then, with a different colored highlighter or pen, have them go through their lines and mark any words that have their sound in it. The skit can be read several times over many days to allow all students to read the various parts.

- As the students rehearse their lines, have them read into a tape recorder. When they listen to themselves, tell them to listen as though they were the audience. Encourage them to make notes on their scripts for any words or phrases they need to say more clearly.

- Allow the students to work on other areas of the production such as backdrops, props, and costumes. This encourages the students to feel ownership of the play, and will further motivate them to make sure the audience understands the dialogue.

- Included at the end of each script is a word list with words from the script that contain the /r/ sound in all contexts. You can use this list to practice in therapy or send it home for additional practice there.

- The activity pages that follow each script are intended for use as extension activities. They are meant to encourage more opportunities for conversational speech practice. Again, these activities can be used in therapy, or sent home for additional practice.

- Have the students create invitations for their parents or another class to come and see the play. Try to find a quiet place for the performance such as the school library. Many times the stage area is in a cafeteria or gymnasium, which makes it very difficult for the audience to hear the dialogue.

The Little Red Rooster

The Little Red Rooster

Characters:
Narrator
Rooster
Ram
Drake

Narrator: There was a little red rooster who lived down the road with his three sons and two friends, Ram and Drake. One day, Rooster noticed a large tree that had been struck by lightning and had fallen to the ground.

Rooster: I bet there's something I can do with this wonderful tree that's fallen. I know! I'll build a fort for my sons. First I'll need to cut the tree. I'll go see if Ram and Drake will help.

(Rooster goes to find his friends.)

Rooster: Ram, Drake, I want to make a fort from the tree that's fallen in our yard. I need someone to help me cut the wood. Can you help?

Ram: I can't! I'm reading a book about the life of the farmer. Sorry, Rooster, but not today.

Drake: Sorry, Rooster. This is my day to rest in the yard. So, I can't today.

Rooster: Well, I guess I'll have to do the work myself.

Narrator: As Rooster began to work on cutting the tree, his three sons came out to help him. They pretended that the tree was an evil burglar come to rob their home, and they attacked him with swords. This made the time go by, and soon the hard work was finished.

Rooster:	Now we must sand the boards to make them smooth so no one gets any splinters. Ram, Drake, will you help us sand the boards?
Ram:	Sorry, Rooster, I can't help you today. I'm supposed to be racing Raccoon this afternoon and I need to stretch and practice my sprint.
Drake:	Oh yeah, right, and I'm the time keeper for the race, so I have to rustle up my stop watch and get ready. We really couldn't possibly help you today.
Rooster:	Oh, then I guess we'll have to do the work by ourselves.
Narrator:	Rooster and his sons began to sand the boards. It was hard work, but they made the time go by faster by using the sand paper to provide rhythm while they sang songs. Soon the boards were smooth and ready to measure for the fort.
Rooster:	Ram! Drake! The boards are ready! Now we need to measure them and decide how large we want the fort. Won't you come help me measure?
Ram:	Ah, Rooster. You know Thursday is our day to play cards. All you do is work, work, work. Don't you want to play cards with us?
Drake:	Yeah, Rooster! Come play cards with us. We can measure the boards later. Playing cards is much more fun.
Rooster:	If we work together, we can have fun too. Playing all the time never gets anything done.
Ram:	Oh, Rooster, you are so boring!
Drake:	Yeah, come on, Ram. Let's go have some fun. I'm afraid we're wasting precious card-playing time!

Narrator: Rooster and his sons were left to do the work alone again. They carefully measured each board and made the plans for their fort. Soon they had all the boards measured, cut and ready to nail together. Rooster tried one last time to get Ram and Drake to help build the fort.

Rooster: OK, guys. This is it. All we have left to do is nail the boards together and our fort will be complete. Are you going to help this time, or not?

Drake: No way, Rooster. Ram and I are going to ride the roller coaster at the fair. Today, they're running it backwards!!

Ram: That's right. We have better things to do than swing a hammer. The Warp Speed ride is waiting for us!

Rooster: OK. I hope you don't get too scared on the roller coaster.

Narrator: So, once again Rooster and his sons had no one to help them do the work. They worked long into the night, but were thrilled when they finally finished their new fort. It was the greatest fort around! The next morning, Ram and Drake rushed to see the new fort.

Ram: Hey, Rooster! This fort is super-great! I can't wait to play soldier-at-war in it! Do you have any swords and rifles?!

Drake: Yeah, Rooster! We can pretend we're pirates hiding from an evil Captain.

Rooster: I'm sorry Ram and Drake, but only those who helped build the fort get to play in it. Anyone who helped cut the tree, sand or measure the boards, or swing a hammer to nail it together is more than welcome to come play in the fort.

Narrator: Rooster and his sons enjoyed playing in their new fort. Before long, however, they looked out and saw Ram and Drake standing sadly by the road.

Rooster: You know, it is good to enjoy the rewards of your hard work. It is better to enjoy them with your friends. Ram, Drake come and play.

Ram: Thanks, Rooster! I'm sorry we didn't help you more when you were building the fort.

Drake: Right, we can see now what a reward it really is when you work together.

The Little Red Rooster

New Vocabulary:

ram   rhythm
drake   measure
fort   moral
resourceful sprint

Comprehension Questions:

1. What did Rooster decide to do with the tree that had fallen in his yard?

2. Why couldn't Ram and Drake help cut the tree?

3. How did Rooster and his sons make the work go faster when they were cutting the wood?

4. What was the next step in building the fort?

5. What did Rooster and his sons do while they were sanding the boards?

6. What did Ram and Drake want Rooster to do instead of measuring the boards?

7. What was the final step in making the fort? What did Ram and Drake decide to do instead?

8. List the steps Rooster and his sons took to make the fort.

9. Think of something you know how to make. What are the steps it takes for you to make it?

10. What was the moral of the story?

The Little Red Rooster

Teacher's Guide

Comprehension Questions:

1. What did Rooster decide to do with the tree that had fallen in his yard?
   He decided to build a fort.

2. Why couldn't Ram and Drake help cut the tree?
   Ram was reading a book. Drake was resting in the yard.

3. How did Rooster and his sons make the work go faster when they were cutting the wood?
   Rooster and his sons pretended the tree was an evil burglar who had come to rob their home and they attacked him with swords.

4. What was the next step in building the fort?
   Sanding the boards

5. What did Rooster and his sons do while they were sanding the boards?
   They used the sand paper to provide rhythm while they sang songs.

6. What did Ram and Drake want Rooster to do instead of measuring the boards?
   Play cards with them

7. What was the final step in making the fort? What did Ram and Drake decide to do instead?
   The final step was nailing the boards together. Ram and Drake went to the fair instead.

8. List the steps Rooster and his sons took to make the fort.
   1. Cut the tree 2. Sand the boards. 3. Measure the boards 4. Nail the fort together

9. Think of something you know how to make. What are the steps it takes for you to make it?
   Answers will vary.

10. What was the moral of the story?
    There is nothing better than getting to enjoy the rewards of your hard work, unless you can enjoy it with your friends.

Language Extensions:
- Sequencing
- Time/Order words
- Compare/Contrast *The Little Red Rooster* with *The Little Red Hen*

The Little Red Rooster

Activity: Write out the steps that Rooster and his sons followed to build the fort below. Then, using your good speech skills, tell a partner about the fort.

Rooster and his sons built a fort with a tree that had fallen in their yard.

First, _____

_____

_____.

Next, _____

_____

_____.

Then, _____

_____

_____.

Finally, _____

_____

_____.

The Little Red Rooster

WORD LIST

INITIAL	INTERNAL and FINAL	BLENDS
red	large	Drake
rooster	fort	tree
road	first	three
Ram	farmer	pretend
reading	work	truly
rest	burglar	stretch
rob	swords	practice
racing	hard	sprint
raccoon	boards	provide
rhythm	splinters	afraid
ready	measure	precious
really	Thursday	tried
ride	together	thrilled
roller coaster	never	greatest
running	boring	friends
rushed	fair	
rifles	backwards	
	hammer	
	warp speed	
	scared	
	morning	
	soldier-at-war	
	pirates	
	better	
	rewards	

Brewster Ryans Cracks the Case

Brewster Ryans Cracks the Case

Characters:

Brewster: 11 year-old super detective
Arbuckle: Brewster's sidekick and best friend
Rudy: Brewster and Arbuckle's neighbor
Rodney: the neighborhood bully

Brewster and Arbuckle are walking down the street deep in conversation.

Brewster: All right, Arbuckle, you're just going to have to try harder. If you're going to be a super detective's sidekick, you have to be able to do this!

Arbuckle: Geez, Brewster! Shouldn't we be studying for a test or riding our bikes or something normal 11-year-olds would be doing? This is crazy!

Brewster: You never know when a skill like this may come in handy! Now try it again!

(Just then, their neighbor, Rudy, comes running up the street.)

Rudy: Brewster! I need your help! Hi, Arbuckle!

Brewster: What seems to be the trouble, Rudy?

Rudy: I was just working on the history report we had for homework, when all of a sudden, it disappeared from my computer screen!

Brewster: Wow! It just disappeared? Hmmm. Sounds like we have a report thief! Did you see anyone walking out with your computer?

Rudy: No, no, Brewster! The computer is still there, but my report isn't!

Arbuckle: Was your monitor still on?

Brewster: Great question, Arbuckle. Did you have a monitor to sound the alarm?

Arbuckle: Not that kind of monitor, Brewster. The computer screen is called the monitor.

Rudy: Yes, the monitor was still on and I could still type, my work was just gone!

Arbuckle: Did you save your work, Rudy?

Brewster: Honestly, Arbuckle! That's why he's come to us, to save his work!

Arbuckle: I mean on the hard drive or a disk!

Rudy: I thought I had, but I may have been wrong. I just can't find it anywhere!

Arbuckle: Were you on the internet when you were working on it, Rudy?

Brewster: You think his work might have got caught in a ne Now that is a strange theory, Arbuckle.

Arbuckle: Good grief, Brewster! Don't you know any thing about computers?

Brewster: Of course I know about computers! I'm the best trained super detective around!

Rudy: You know, Arbuckle, I think I was on the internet. Could that mean something?

Arbuckle: Well, it depends. Was there another computer that was networked to yours through the internet? If someone wanted to steal your work, that would be one way they could do it.

Brewster: Of course, Arbuckle! I had already thought of that. Now the question is, who would want to steal your report, Rudy?

Rudy: Well, that bully, Rodney, is in my class. He plays football and they told him if he didn't get a better grade on this report, he wouldn't get to play for the rest of the tournament. He's already been suspended from two games.

Brewster: Aha! Well that seems like reason enough to me! Let's go find Rodney and see what he is up to!

The three boys see Rodney down the street beating up on three young kids.

Rodney: Right ! You three better have the Red Rocketman tomorrow!

The children run off.

Brewster: Well, well, Rodney. Picking on the little guys again, I see. Are you scared of kids your own size?

Rodney: Well, I'm certainly not scared of you, Brewster! You want to go a few rounds with me, or are you a coward?

Brewster: I'm afraid we don't have the time right now, Rodney. We're on a case. Someone has run off with Rudy's history report. Do you know anything about that, Rodney?

Rodney: What? Are you trying to call me a robber? I haven't run off with anything! Certainly not a history report! I hate history!

Brewster: Exactly! That is why you would hate having to write the report and would prefer to steal it from Rudy!

Rodney: How dare you, Brewster? I didn't steal anything! Right, Arbuckle? Arbuckle will tell you I was with him last night!

Arbuckle: Ummm. Yes, he was with me. We were working hard on a project.

Rodney: There! I told you! A project with my great friend Arbuckle!

Brewster: But, Arbuckle, you and Rodney don't have any classes together. What kind of project would you have to work on?

Rodney: Slow down, Brewster. You're not letting Nerd-Boy answer! Go ahead, Arbuckle.

Arbuckle: Well, it was for the…umm…football team…yeah! They asked me to write a story for the newspaper and I had to interview Rodney.

Rodney: Right! I was busy answering all his interview questions when that report was stolen, so it couldn't have been me! Besides, how in the world do you expect me to sneak into Rudy's house when the little nerd is there every night?!

Rudy: The report was stolen directly from my computer. You wouldn't have had to be in my house.

Rodney: Well, that proves it! I hate computers as much as I hate history! I am certainly not a nerd like you three!

Brewster: Well, I guess we'll have to look somewhere else. Arbuckle, Rudy, let's go.

The three leave Rodney.

Brewster: All right, Arbuckle, you are up to something and I want to know what!

Arbuckle: What do you mean, Brewster?

Rudy: Yeah, Brewster, Arbuckle wouldn't take my report. He's not in my history class and he could write a better report than me any day!

Brewster: That may be so, but he and Rodney are lying and I can prove it!

Rudy: How?

Brewster: First of all, we never told Rodney the report was stolen last night, so how did he know to come up with an alibi for that exact time? Second, Rodney has been suspended from football because of his grade in history, so why would Arbuckle be interviewing him for an article about the football team?

Rudy: Hmmm, that is kind of strange, Arbuckle.

Arbuckle: Oh, you guys! Rodney was blackmailing me. He somehow discovered my work on the relationship between organic carrots and processed carrots and their effect on rabbits. He stole all my research. He was holding it for ransom if I didn't get him an A on his history report.

Rudy: But why would you take my report?

Arbuckle: Well, Rudy, I'm not in your history class, for one thing, and Rodney had no idea what the report was supposed to be about. You're the only person I was sure would get an A on that report. Plus, I thought you had saved it so it wouldn't really hurt you.

Brewster: Well, you should know, Arbuckle, that I will always find the culprit!

Rudy: But, Arbuckle, I still don't understand how you got into my computer.

Arbuckle: You're always logged onto the internet, so the last time I was at your house playing Warcraft, I just shared your files onto the network. All I needed was your IP address and I was able to get to everything I needed.

Brewster: All you need is someone's address and you can get into their house through their computer?!

Arbuckle: No, the IP address is the computer's address on the internet. It has nothing to do with your house address, Brewster. I was only able to get to things that Rudy had on his computer.

Rudy: Wow! I guess I should protect my work a little better in the future.

Arbuckle: I'm really sorry, Rudy. I really didn't mean to hurt you.

Rudy: No, I understand, Arbuckle. Rodney can be a pretty scary guy!

Arbuckle: He is scary, but it was still my decision to do the wrong thing. My research was important to me, but it shouldn't have been more important than knowing the right thing and doing it. That's what having good character is all about. Our character is one thing Rodney can't steal from us, unless we let him.

Brewster: Well, once we take our proof, and your testimony, to the principal, Rodney will probably want to stay away from us for a while!

Rudy: I know I'll want to stay away from him!

Arbuckle: That's for sure!

Brewster Ryans Cracks the Case

New Vocabulary:

monitor	organic	character
network	culprit	
internet	IP address	

Comprehension Questions:

1. What is Rudy's problem?

2. Brewster misunderstands Arbuckle because he is thinking of different meanings for the words Arbuckle is using. What did Arbuckle mean, and what did Brewster think he meant, for these words: monitor, save, internet, IP address.

3. Why did Rudy consider Rodney a suspect?

4. Why did Rodney say he couldn't have been the one to steal Rudy's report?

5. How did Brewster know he was lying?

6. How was Rodney blackmailing Arbuckle?

7. How did Arbuckle steal Rudy's report?

8. What is the one thing no one can steal from us?

9. What would have been a better solution to Arbuckle's problem?

10. At the beginning of the play, Brewster and Arbuckle are practicing an important super detective skill. What do you think it might have been?

Brewster Ryans Cracks the Case

Teacher's Guide

Comprehension Questions:

1. What is Rudy's problem?
    His history report was stolen from his computer.

2. Brewster misunderstands Arbuckle because he is thinking of different meanings for the words Arbuckle is using. What did Arbuckle mean, and what did Brewster think he meant, for these words: monitor, save, internet, IP address.
    Monitor: Arbuckle meant a computer monitor. Brewster thought he meant to monitor something, as in to observe, or keep track of, something.
    Save: Arbuckle meant to save work onto a computer disk or hard drive. Brewster thought he meant to save it, as in to rescue it.
    Internet: Arbuckle was referring to the internet available through a computer that links you to things like the World Wide Web. Brewster thought he was talking about a net that something might get caught in.
    IP address: Arbuckle was talking about the computer's address on the World Wide Web. Brewster thought he was talking about someone's home address.

3. Why did Rudy consider Rodney a suspect?
    Rodney was not a good student and had to get a good grade on this report to be able to play football. He was also a bully and wasn't a very nice person.

4. Why did Rodney say he couldn't have been the one to steal Rudy's report?
    He said that Arbuckle was interviewing him for the school newspaper.

5. How did Brewster know he was lying?
    Rodney knew what time Rudy's paper was stolen even though Brewster had not told him and he was suspended from the football team for bad grades so it wouldn't make sense for him to be interviewing him about the team..

6. How was Rodney blackmailing Arbuckle?
    He had stolen Arbuckle's scientific research, and told him he would keep it if Arbuckle didn't get him an A on his history paper.

7. How did Arbuckle steal Rudy's report?
   He contacted Rudy's computer through the internet.

8. What is the one thing no one can steal from us?
   Our character.

9. What would have been a better solution to Arbuckle's problem?
   Talking with an adult, such as one of his parents or a teacher.

10. At the beginning of the play, Brewster and Arbuckle are practicing an important super detective skill. What do you think it might have been?
    Answers will vary. Encourage the students to be creative!

Language Extensions:
- Multiple meaning words
- Non-literal language
- Dealing with problems/bullies

Brewster Ryans Cracks the Case

Activity: Use the comic strip below to retell the story. Cut the pictures apart and add captions for each frame. Remember to use your good speech skills!

25

Brewster Ryans Cracks the Case
WORD LIST

INITIAL	INTERNAL and FINAL	BLENDS
Ryan	Arbuckle	Brewster
Rudy	conversation	cracks
Rodney	harder	try
riding	super	crazy
report	normal	trouble
wrong	working	screen
rest	history	drive
Red Rocketman	disappeared	strange
rounds	computer	trained
run	monitor	prefer
robber	alarm	proudly
write	hard	project
right	anywhere	proves
relationship	theory	grade
rabbits	internet	principal
ransom	networked	afraid
wrong	better	Warcraft
	tournament	
	scared	
	certainly	
	coward	
	dare	
	nerd-boy	
	answer	
	newspaper	
	interview	
	directly	
	somewhere	
	article	
	discovered	
	organic	
	carrots	
	hurt	
	culprit	
	Warcraft	
	important	
	character	

Rhonda's Surprise Party

Rhonda's Surprise Party

Characters:
Rhonda - A girl having her 12th birthday
Audrey - Rhonda's best friend
Aaron - A friend from school
Brandi – Another friend from school
Mr. Shepherd - Owner of the pet store
Mother - Rhonda's mother

Rhonda and Audrey are in Rhonda's bedroom after school on Monday.

Audrey: So, Rhonda. What do you think you're getting this year for your birthday?

Rhonda: Well, I'm think I'm getting something pretty large, because Mother had to clean out a space in the garage the other day!

Audrey: Really? Do you think it's a scooter?

Rhonda: Oh, maybe. I've been hoping for a certain something I saw in town on Thursday.

Audrey: Like a dress? Where were you? A department store?

Rhonda: Well, Mother and I were on our way to visit her friend, and we passed Shepherd's Pet Store. I saw a precious red puppy in the window, and I told Mother I thought I wanted him for my birthday.

Audrey: Oh, cool! What would you name him?

Rhonda: I think either Rover or Rusty!

Audrey: Oh, those are hard to choose between!

Rhonda: Well, I probably better not count my chickens before they hatch!

The next day at school, in the cafeteria. Rhonda, Audrey, Aaron, and Brandi are talking..

Brandi: Hey, Rhonda, Audrey says you might get a puppy for a birthday present!

Rhonda: Yes! I might get a dog. I also might not.

Aaron: Well, if you do get one, what will you name her?

Rhonda:	Wrong! Not her, him! The one I want is a boy.
Audrey:	And she really wants to name him Rover or Rusty.
Aaron:	Oh, my brother's best friend is named Rusty. Well, not really, but we call him that because his hair is red.
Rhonda:	This puppy's hair is red too! I think it's a Labrador retriever, but I'm not sure.
Brandi:	Maybe we could all go to Shepherd's and see it! Do you think we could get permission from our parents to go this afternoon?
Aaron:	Probably! I don't have any homework! Let's try it!

Outside Shepherd's Pet Store window that afternoon.

Rhonda:	Oh, isn't he just adorable?
Brandi:	He is a pretty little thing!
Audrey:	I know! He's precious!
Aaron:	I don't know why you girls are so crazy over him. He looks like just an ordinary puppy to me!

(They all laugh. Mr. Shepherd comes outside to sweep the walk.)

Mr. Shepherd:	Hi, children! How are you this afternoon?
All four kids:	Great!
Rhonda:	Mr. Shepherd, how old is that cute red puppy right there?
Mr. Shepherd:	Well, let's see, Rhonda. He's right at three months old, I believe.
Audrey:	Oh, that's perfect!
Aaron:	How is that perfect, Audrey?
Audrey:	Well, he's old enough to leave his mother and still young enough to be rowdy and playful. Right, Mr. Shepherd?
Mr. Shepherd:	That's right, Audrey. Very good.
Brandi:	Well, Mr. Shepherd, what price are you asking for the puppy?
Aaron:	Is he real expensive?
Mr. Shepherd:	He's only thirty dollars, children. Are you wanting to buy him?
Brandi:	Thirty dollars!!! That's more money than the four of us have put together!

(They all laugh.)

Aaron:	Maybe we'll come back another time when we can afford him.
All four kids:	Bye, Mr. Shepherd!!

Wednesday morning in the hall outside of class. Audrey, Aaron, and Brandi are alone.

Audrey:	Hi, guys! Did you get my e-mail last night about Operation-Rhonda?
Brandi:	Yeah, I love it! My mother says I have permission, so just alert me when you're ready.
Aaron:	Me too. My mother gave me the "OK" so I'm ready when you girls are.

(Rhonda walks up.)

Rhonda:	Good morning, you guys. Did anyone have trouble with their math project? It was a lot harder than I originally thought it was going to be!!
Audrey:	Oh, yes. I think Mr. Brown does that on purpose so that we can't even relax at home!
Brandi:	Seriously! I didn't even get to see my favorite TV program last night because of that last word problem.
Aaron:	We had homework?

Thursday afternoon in Rhonda's bedroom.

Brandi:	So, do you still think your mother might buy the red puppy, Rhonda?
Rhonda:	Well, maybe, but I'm really starting to doubt it.
Audrey:	Why? What's wrong?
Rhonda:	Yesterday, my father put a new riding lawn mower in the area Mother cleaned out in the garage. So, now I'm sure that wasn't for my present.

Both Audrey and Brandi: Oh, sorry.

Rhonda:	That's all right. There's still hope.
Brandi:	That's right! I hope you stay cheerful, because you just never know what's around the corner for you!!
Rhonda:	Well, remember when I said that I'd probably have my party on Saturday? I found out for sure, and I want to invite you two first!
Brandi:	Woo-hoo!!! I adore parties!! What's the plan?
Audrey:	And what should we wear?!
Rhonda:	Okay, it's going to be Saturday at three in the afternoon, right here in my living room. I know it's short notice, but since I just got the approval last night, I couldn't tell you until now.

Audrey and Brandi: Oh no!

Rhonda:	What's wrong?
Audrey:	My grandmother is coming to visit Saturday afternoon. I was thinking you'd have the party that night so I wasn't worried before.
Brandi:	Right, and I'm supposed to be taking care of my little brother that afternoon while my parents visit my grandfather in the nursing home.
Rhonda:	So neither of you can come?
Audrey:	I'm sorry, Rhonda!
Brandi:	Yeah, Rhonda, I'm so sorry! But I'll bring over a present that night for you, OK?
Audrey:	Right! Me too!!

That evening in Rhonda's living room. Rhonda is alone. The phone rings.

Rhonda:	Hello?
Aaron:	Hi, Rhonda, it's Aaron.
Rhonda:	Hi, Aaron! I'm so glad you're calling me!
Aaron:	Well, you're probably not going to be real happy when I tell you the reason.
Rhonda:	Oh, no. Don't say it!
Aaron:	Well, I talked to my parents about your birthday party, and they refuse to let me come.
Rhonda:	Really? Why not?
Aaron:	Because, the last time I went to a party, I left without asking permission and they were really worried. They said I would have to miss out on the next party, only, they didn't know that it would be a party for you! They say they are real sorry, but they have to stand firm.
Rhonda:	Rats, Aaron! Audrey and Brandi can't come either! This is terrible!

Aaron:	I'm really sorry, Rhonda. But my parents promised that I could bring my present to you at church on Sunday morning. And it's really neat. I think you'll like it.
Rhonda:	OK. Thanks, Aaron. I understand. I'll see you tomorrow at school.
Aaron:	All right. Well, bye.
Rhonda:	Bye.

Friday in the cafeteria at school. All four sit at a table.

Aaron:	Hey, did any of you girls understand Mr. Peterman's lesson about frogs today?
Audrey:	Well, I think he was mainly talking about their differences.
Brandi:	Or their similarities, you know, like how they relate to each other.
Aaron:	What are you taking about?
Audrey:	We're talking about the presentation he gave. Weren't you paying attention?
Aaron:	Sort of. I mean, I wrote some notes. Here, let me show you.

(Aaron pulls out his notebook and stares at a piece of paper.)

Aaron:	Er….well, never mind.
Brandi:	What's wrong? What did you write down?
Aaron:	I started taking notes. I guess I just drifted off after a certain point.
Audrey:	What certain point? I mean, you at least wrote some important stuff down, right?
Aaron:	Here's what I wrote. "Mr. Peterman: Frog."
Brandi:	That's the entire page?
Audrey:	That's all you have?
Aaron:	Apparently so.

(All three laugh, but then notice that Rhonda has been quiet the entire time.)

Brandi: Hey, Rhonda. What's the matter?

Rhonda: Oh, nothing. I am just trying to not be upset about no one coming to my party tomorrow.

Audrey: Oh, that's right. But we'll have a party for you another time! I promise!

Rhonda: I know, that's what my mom said, too. Thanks.

Rhonda is at Shepherd's Pet Store that afternoon.

Rhonda: Well, maybe seeing Rusty/Rover will cheer me up.

Mr. Shepherd: Hello, Rhonda. What brings you over today?

Rhonda: I was hoping to see that adorable red retriever, Mr. Shepherd.

Mr. Shepherd: Oh, dear. I'm sorry! I sold the retriever. Just this morning, in fact.

Rhonda: What? Great! What else can go wrong?

Saturday morning.

Rhonda: Morning, Mother. Is it okay if I just eat my cereal in my room upstairs?

Mother: Sure, Rhonda. I'm sorry none of your friends could make it this afternoon.

Rhonda: That's all right. I know they really wanted to.

Mother: Well, you go enjoy a quiet morning to yourself, and I'll start baking your birthday cake. We'll just have a quiet celebration with your father, and I promise you'll have a great time!

Rhonda: OK.

Noon at Rhonda's house. Rhonda's mother knocks on the door to Rhonda's room.

Mother: Rhonda? Are you OK?

Rhonda: Yes. I'm just listening to the radio and pretending that it's not my birthday. You can come in.

Mother: Pretending it's not your birthday? Oh, that's discouraging.

Rhonda: No, it's making me feel better.

Mother: But it's certainly too bad. Your father and I have something pretty special for you downstairs. But if it's not your birthday, I guess we'll have to return it.

Rhonda: Really? You have something for me?

Mother: Of course! Why don't you close your eyes and let me lead you downstairs to see!

Rhonda: OK!

Everyone but Rhonda: SURPRISE!!!!!

Rhonda: Wow! What in the world are you guys doing here?!

Aaron: Celebrating your birthday with a surprise party!! Did we really surprise you?

Rhonda:	Yes! You certainly did!! I thought you all really had plans and wouldn't be arriving until tonight!!
Brandi:	Well, we started to feel cruel about it yesterday in the cafeteria when you were so sad, but it was worth it to see your surprised reaction!!
Audrey:	Happy Birthday, Rhonda. I hope you're not angry with us.
Rhonda:	Of course not! This is the greatest birthday ever!!
Aaron:	That's a relief. I figured you might throw us out!
Rhonda:	Never!
Mother:	Well, kids. I think this would be a good time to give Rhonda the present you brought.
Brandi:	Right!! OK, Rhonda close your eyes one more time.
Rhonda:	OK! This is really exciting!!

(Rhonda closes her eyes and they put the red puppy in her arms. The puppy starts licking her face and she opens her eyes and squeals!)

Rhonda:	Rusty/Rover! You're really here!!!!
Aaron:	Rusty/Rover?
Rhonda:	Yes. I refuse to decide on either name. I'll just call him both.

(They all laugh.)

Rhonda's Surprise Party

New Vocabulary:
precious
Labrador retriever
rowdy
alert
adore

Comprehension Questions:

1. What special day are Rhonda and her friends getting ready for?

2. What clue makes Rhonda think her parents are getting her something big for her birthday?

3. What does Rhonda really want for her birthday?

4. What does Rhonda mean when she says, "I probably better not count my chickens before they hatch."

5. Why does Audrey think three months is the best age for a puppy?

6. What is "Operation Rhonda"?

7. What excuses did Audrey, Brandi, and Aaron have for missing Rhonda's party?

8. What does Rhonda do on the day of her birthday to make herself feel better?

9. Why was Audrey worried that Rhonda might be angry about the surprise party?

10. Tell about one of your favorite birthdays. What would happen on your perfect birthday?

Rhonda's Surprise Party

Teacher's Guide

Comprehension Questions:

1. What special day are Rhonda and her friends getting ready for?
   Rhonda's birthday.

2. What clue makes Rhonda think her parents are getting her something big for her birthday?
   Her mother made room for something big in the garage.

3. What does Rhonda really want for her birthday?
   A puppy.

4. What does Rhonda mean when she says, "I better not count my chickens before they hatch."
   Don't count on something before you know that it's going to happen.

5. Why does Audrey think three months is the best age for a puppy?
   The puppy is old enough to leave his mother, but still young enough to be playful.

6. What is "Operation Rhonda"?
   The plan for the surprise party.

7. What excuses did Audrey, Brandi, and Aaron have for missing Rhonda's party?
   Audrey's grandmother was coming to visit, Brandi had to babysit her brother and Aaron was grounded.

8. What does Rhonda do on the day of her birthday to make herself feel better?
   She pretends it's not her birthday.

9. Why was Audrey worried that Rhonda might be angry about the surprise party?
   She was afraid Rhonda would think they were mean.

10. Tell about one of your favorite birthdays. What would be your perfect birthday?
    Answers will vary.

Language Extensions:
- Idioms
- Pragmatic language: birthday party
- Oral grammar

Rhonda's Surprise Party

Activity: In this skit, Rhonda's friends planned a great surprise for Rhonda. In the space below write about a birthday party you have had, or would like to have. Then, using your good speech skills, tell a partner all about it!

Rhonda's Surprise Party

WORD LIST

INITIAL	INTERNAL and FINAL	BLENDS
Rhonda	Aaron	Audrey
really	Mr. Shepherd	Brandi
red	mother	dress
Rover	year	friend
Rusty	birthday	precious
wrong	garage	present
rowdy	scooter	probably
right	Thursday	try
real	department	great
relax	store	proce
riding	hard	trouble
remember	cafeteria	Mr. Brown
right	Labrador Retriever	approval
reason	permission	grandmother
refuse	adorable	grandfather
Mr. Peterson's	ordinary	bring
wrote	children	crazy
return	perfect	pretty
relief	thirty	frogs
	dollars	presentation
	four	drifted
	together	promise
	afford	celebration
	alert	surprise
	favorite	cruel
	word	angry
	homework	
	mower	
	cheerful	
	never	
	corner	
	Saturday	
	father	
	party	
	wear	
	afternoon	
	worried	
	parents	
	aware	
	firm	
	cereal	

The Incredible Shrinking Twins

The Incredible Shrinking Twins

Characters:

Terrance
Tracy
Roscoe

Dr. Raymond's lab

Terrance: When did Dr. Raymond say he would be arriving at work?

Tracy: Three o'clock, I think. We're really early.

Terrance: I wonder what he'll want from us today.

Tracy: Well, he said he's about to wrap up his research on twins. Maybe this will be our last meeting.

Terrance: Oh, I hope not! I love our talks with Dr. Raymond. Maybe we can find another experiment for him to try on us.

Tracy: Oh, super idea, Terrance! Let's take a quick look around the laboratory and see what we can come up with.

Terrance: Great! Oooh, Tracy! Check out this green stuff! It sort of looks like the sherbet we had for dessert last night.

Tracy: Yummy! Too bad it isn't. Terrance, what on earth are you trying to do?

Terrance: Well, I just wanted to know if it had the same odor as the sherbet.

Tracy: Be careful! You're about to spill it all over the counter!

Terrance spills green liquid.

Terrance: Gross! Tracy, help me! I've made a royal mess.

Tracy: What a disaster! Dr. Raymond is going to murder us!

Terrance: Be sure to get every drop. This stuff is greasy. Yuck!

Tracy: Oh, gross! I got it on me! Terrance, grab a rag and help me wipe it off!

Terrance: Well, all right. But I have it all over my arm and wrist.

Tracy: Terrance, I really don't feel well. I wonder if I'm allergic to this stuff.

Terrance: That's probably it, Tracy. You're allergic to everything! However, I'm not allergic to anything, and I'm starting to feel weird too.

Tracy: Oh, something very strange is happening. My ears are ringing!

Terrance: My ears are ringing too! We've got a bigger problem than that though, Tracy.

Tracy: What are you talking about? I think ringing ears is a pretty large problem!

Terrance: Well, large is precisely the right word here. Everything in Dr. Raymond's laboratory just got a lot bigger!

Tracy: No, Terrance! We're getting smaller!

Terrance: You're right! What are we going to do?

Tracy: Well, first of all, we stay calm. Second, we try to figure out how to stop shrinking. Third, we find Dr. Raymond!

Terrance: Really? In that precise order? Because I'm ready to find Dr. Raymond right away!

Tracy: Yes, Terrance. First we calm down. And look! We're not shrinking anymore! The process seems to be over.

Terrance: So now can we find Dr. Raymond? Please?

A ringing noise sounds above them and they look up.

Terrance: Um…Tracy? Did you hear that?

Tracy: Yeah. I wonder what it is. It seems to be coming from the counter. Wait a minute, Terrance. Did you leave your cell phone up there?

Terrance: Yes! That's it! I had the alarm on it set when we were hoping to meet with Dr. Raymond. It'll just ring three times and then stop.

Tracy: Wonderful! Perhaps someone will hear it and come to rescue us!

Terrance: Dr. Raymond should be here any second now, too. That ring means it's time.

Roscoe: Remember, Dr. Raymond went to a convention on molecular restructuring. He won't be back until four o'clock.

Tracy: Terrance, did we go crazy as well as shrink?
It sounded as if that parrot was talking to us.

Terrance: No, it must just be another of Dr. Raymond's illusions. Parrots don't talk, they only mimic.

Roscoe: You just shrank to three inches tall and you have trouble believing that a parrot can talk?

Terrance: OK, you have a point there.

Roscoe: I was one of Dr. Raymond's successful experiments. My name is Roscoe.

Tracy: Nice to meet you, Roscoe.

Terrance: Um, do you think you could help us?

Roscoe: Unfortunately, I'm locked up in this cage. There's not a lot I can do.

Terrance: OK, well let's just try to problem solve this situation. Whatever we do, we have to figure out a way to contact Dr. Raymond. Even if he does come here, he won't be able to find us, as little as we are. We have to figure out a way to let him know we're down here.

Tracy: I think the trick is to get to the cell phone. If we could find a way to reach the top of the table, then we could call Dr. Raymond and tell him what's happened.

Terrance: I was thinking the same thing. I just can't figure out how to get to the top of the table.

Roscoe: He won't have his cell phone on during the convention.

Tracy: Hmmm, that is a problem, but, he may have it on vibrate.

Terrance: If not, we'll just have to leave him a message and hope he gets it sooner rather than later.

Tracy: But how are we going to get to the cell phone?

Terrance: Well let's look around. Seeing things through our new eyes may help us to find a way around this problem.

Tracy: Hey! Look over there! It looks like Dr. Raymond was changing out the air conditioner filter and left the grate out. It's leaning against the table. I bet we could climb that grate, Terrance.

Terrance: Yeah, I think we could. It doesn't reach all the way to the top, though. How will we get from the top of the grate to the top of the table?

Tracy: Well, the computer cable is pretty close to the grate. Maybe once we got up there, we could balance each other so we could reach out and grab that cable. Then we could use it to brace ourselves as we climb up the wall of the desk.

Terrance: I really don't think we could reach it. It just looks too far away. Maybe there is something around we could use to help us reach a little farther and hook it.

Tracy: Maybe we could find, a paperclip or something.

Roscoe: A paperclip would be too big. Trust me, I know about these things. You could carry it, but you wouldn't be able to balance it well enough to reach out and hook the cable.

Tracy:	Hey! What about this staple? It isn't big at all. It must have come out of Dr. Raymond's bulletin board up there. It hasn't been bent at all.
Terrance:	Yeah, I think that might work. Here, I'll hook it to my belt loop so we can use both hands to climb the grate.
Roscoe:	If I wasn't in this cage, I could just fly down there and lift you guys to the table. I don't know why Dr. Raymond doesn't trust me when he's gone.
Tracy:	He probably trusts you. It is just that this lab is dangerous. Look what happened to us while he was gone!
Roscoe:	You're probably right. I just hate not being able to help you kids.
Terrance:	It's just nice to know there's another pair of eyes watching out for trouble!
Roscoe:	And I can certainly do that!
Tracy:	OK, Terrance. Let's get started. The sooner we start this climb, the better.
Terrance:	Too bad I didn't wear my hiking boots today.
Tracy:	Yes, too bad you didn't have the foresight to realize we were going to be climbing a grate to get to the top of a desk so we could reach a cell phone to call Dr. Raymond and tell him we have been shrunk to only three inches high. Next time, Terrance, you will just have to try harder.
Terrance:	Boy, do you sound bitter! Feeling a little stressed?
Tracy:	I don't know why I would!

Roscoe: OK, you two. Remember your first step, Tracy? Calm down. It will be OK. I have seen Dr. Raymond shrink tons of things and they have all turned out just fine. Granted he's never done a person before, and the rabbit he shrunk last week did have very small ears for a while, but in the end, he always figures it out.

Terrance: Roscoe, I don't think that helped.

Tracy: Oh, let's just get this over with! Do you think this grate will hold us?

Terrance: Sure. Remember, we are only three inches high. How much could we weigh?

Tracy: True. Well, why don't you go first and I'll come behind you, since you have the staple.

Terrance:	OK, but be careful. Wow! This grate is a lot stronger than it looked. This isn't very hard to climb at all!
Tracy:	Speak for yourself. You're not the one who's scared of heights.
Terrance:	Oh, Tracy, I forgot. You know there really isn't any reason for us both to climb up here. You could probably just wait on the ground.
Tracy:	Wait down there for some spider or rodent or something to spot me? No thanks!
Terrance:	Well then, just keep your eyes on me and don't look down.
Tracy:	Why do people always say that? You know all it makes me want to do is look down!
Terrance:	OK, I'm at the top. Now I just need to get to the staple. Oh no! I dropped it! Tracy do you see it?
Roscoe:	I see it, Tracy. It's just to your right.
Tracy:	Yes, it's hooked on the grate. Hang on, I think I can get it. Here, I got it. I will bring it up to you.
Roscoe:	Be careful, Tracy.
Tracy:	Here you go, Terrance. See if you can get the cable.
Terrance:	Mmmm, I got it! Now here, Tracy. You take the staple so you can get the cable after I'm up.
Tracy:	OK. Be careful, Terrance.

Terrance: Ooh. OK this part's not so easy. They make scaling a wall look so easy on TV. OK, left foot, hand, right foot…almost there. Remind me to thank mom for those gymnastics classes. OK, I'm here. Tracy, it is really tricky, are you sure you want to try it?

Tracy: Hey, I was much better than you in gymnastics. If you can do it, I can do it.

Roscoe: Really, Tracy, be careful!!

Tracy: I got it. I'm almost there. Whoa!

Terrance: Here, grab my hand! OK, I got you.

Tracy: Whew! OK, that was a little scary! Now where's the cell phone?

Roscoe: Over there at the edge of the desk. It's right beside that can of Dr. Pepper.

Terrance: Oh! I see it. OK, Roscoe, what's the number?

Roscoe: 3-9-4 9-3-4-3. Tell me when it is ringing.

Tracy: Hang on, Roscoe. We can't jump that fast. 3-9-4—what?

Roscoe: 9-3-4-3.

Terrance: OK. I hear it ringing, Tracy. I will tell you when Dr. Raymond answers.

Tracy: Oh! I hope he has it on silent!

Terrance: OK, Tracy! Talk!

Tracy: Dr. Raymond! Dr. Raymond! This is Tracy Thurman. We are in your lab and we have been shrunk!

Terrance: He hears you! He says, "Ummm, don't touch anything." He wants to know if we are OK. He's at a convention in Colorado!!

Roscoe: Oops. I only knew he was at a convention. I didn't know it was in Colorado.

Tracy: Oh no! Yes, we are OK. Terrance is listening to you on one end of the phone, and I'm here at the other. We had to climb up a grate and then scale the desk to get up here to the cell phone. Roscoe helped us.

Roscoe: Uh oh. Now I'm in trouble.

Terrance: No, no. Dr. Raymond says he's glad you were here. He says he wished he hadn't shut the cage. He wants to know what we were doing in his lab.

Tracy: Dr. Raymond, we were hoping with you today. We wanted to talk to you about your research on twins. We accidentally knocked over some green, gooey stuff, and when we tried to clean it up, we shrunk. We didn't mean to.

Terrance: He says he's sorry he is not here. Umm…he says to look for the antidote. It is the red, gooey stuff here on the desk. Do you see it?

Roscoe: I see it! It is at the other end by the coffee mug.

Terrance: He says not to open it until we are off the desk. It's fast acting.

Tracy: How are we going to get it off the desk?

Terrance: Well, we could just push it off the edge and then climb down to it. That might help open it too!

Tracy: Well, we could give it a try.

Terrance: OK, here. Push.

Tracy: Good, now let's climb down to it, fast!

Terrance: No, not fast. We still need to be careful. I think getting down will be even harder than getting up.

Tracy: No way! We can just slide down the cable until we hit the grate. The grate was easy. Watch!

Terrance: Hey, that looks like fun! OK. Here I come!

Tracy: Now where did the goo fall?

Terrance: Over there! Come on!

Tracy: It looks like the lid popped off when it hit that pen on the ground. Let's rub it on our arms, like we did the green goo, and see if it works.

Terrance: I'm feeling that funny feeling again.

Tracy: Me too. Oh! It's working, Terrance! You're growing.

Terrance: You are too, Tracy! Whew! I am so glad! Hurry! Let's get to the cell phone and tell Dr. Raymond.

Tracy: OK, and ask him what he thinks we should do with a three foot tall pen.

Terrance: What? Oh my goodness, the goo fell on the pen! It grew too! Ha ha! Now that would make an interesting gift at an office party!

The Incredible Shrinking Twins

New Vocabulary:

experiment	process	foresight
laboratory	conference	bitter
sherbet	illusion	rodent
allergic	mimic	research
shrink	vibrate	antidote
precise	grate	

Comprehension Questions:

1. Why were Tracy and Terrance in Dr. Raymond's laboratory? Why did they start looking around?

2. What happened when they spilled the green goo?

3. Who was Roscoe?

4. What plan did Tracy and Terrance come up with to try to contact Dr. Raymond?

5. How were Tracy and Terrance able to use the phone?

6. What did Dr. Raymond tell them to do to solve the problem?

7. What souvenir did Tracy and Terrance end up with at the end of the play?

8. If you could be three inches high for a day, what would you do?

9. If you had a talking parrot, what do you think it would say?

10. If you were a research scientist, what would you want to research?

Language Extensions:
- Analogies
- Problem solving
- Verbal reasoning

The Incredible Shrinking Twins

Teacher's Guide:

Comprehension Questions:

1. Why were Tracy and Terrance in Dr. Raymond's laboratory? Why did they start looking around?
   Dr. Raymond was doing research on twins.

2. What happened when they spilled the green goo?
   They shrunk.

3. Who was Roscoe?
   A talking parrot in Dr. Raymond's laboratory.

4. What plan did Tracy and Terrance come up with to try to contact Dr. Raymond?
   They would climb the air conditioning grate to get to the cell phone on the desk.

5. How were Tracy and Terrance able to use the phone?
   Terrance jumped on the numbers. Tracy talked while Terrance listened.

6. What did Dr. Raymond tell them to do to solve the problem?
   Use the red goo.

7. What souvenir did Tracy and Terrance end up with at the end of the play?
   A three-foot-tall pen.

8. If you could be three inches high for a day, what would you do?
   Answers will vary.

9. If you had a talking parrot, what do you think it would say?
   Answers will vary.

10. If you were a research scientist, what would you want to research?
    Answers will vary.

Language Extensions:
- Analogies
- Problem solving
- Verbal reasoning

The Incredible Shrinking Twins

Activity: Tracy and Terrance were shrunk to three inches tall. What would you do if you could be three inches tall for a day? What kind of dangers would you face? Write a paragraph below about your adventures, and then use your good speech skills to tell a partner all about it!

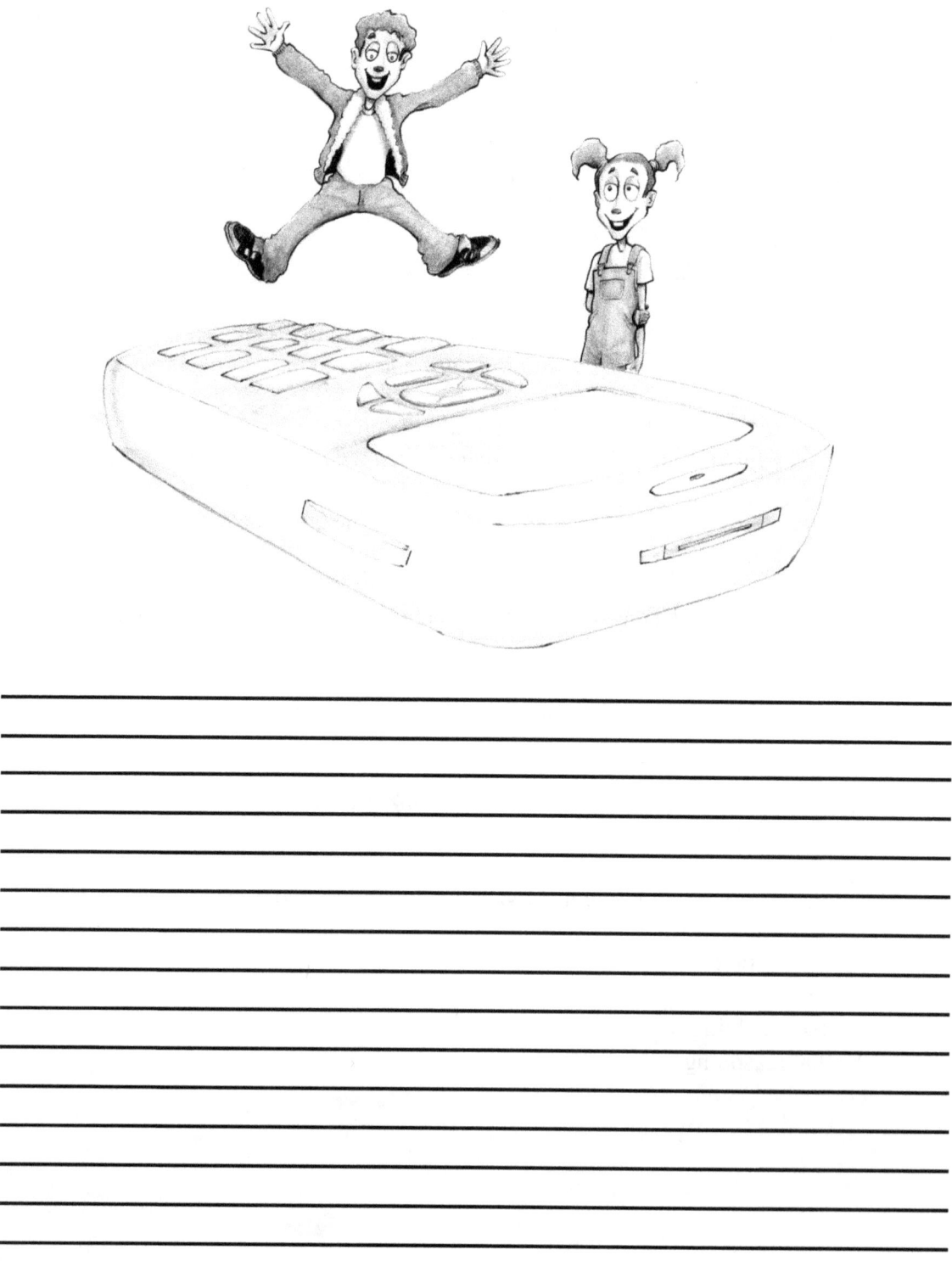

_____
_____
_____
_____
_____
_____
_____
_____
_____
_____
_____
_____

The Incredible Shrinking Twins

WORD LIST

INITIAL	INTERNAL and FINAL	BLENDS
Roscoe	Terrance	incredible
Raymond	arrive	shrinking
research	work	Tracy
rag	early	green
wrist	doctor	trying
ringing	experiment	gross
right	laboratory	drop
reach	sherbet	greasy
rabbit	earth	growing
remember	odor	strange
rub	counter	process
	disaster	trouble
	murder	problem
	arm	trick
	allergic	vibrate
	ears	through
	everything	grate
	bigger	brace
	smaller	trust
	hear	shrunk
	alarm	stressed
	conference	stronger
	parrot	dropped
	computer	bring
	farther	grab
	paperclip	
	carry	
	board	
	work	
	dangerous	
	foresight	
	bitter	
	hard	
	Dr. Pepper	
	answers	
	Colorado	
	sorry	
	other	
	careful	
	hurry	
	interesting	

Rachel Runs the Race

RACHEL RUNS THE RACE

Characters:

Robert—a fifth grade boy on the track team
Robin—a fifth grade girl on the track team
Rachel—a new fifth grade girl who just moved to town

Robert: Hey Robin! Are you going to run in the relay race this weekend?

Robin: Man, Robert, I wish I could, but the doctor said I'm going to have to rest before I can run in the relay race again. I hurt my right ankle pretty badly in last week's race.

Robert: Oh no! And this week's race is against Rock Hill. They always beat us!

Robin: I know, and their lead runner, Richard, is a real jerk! When they beat us last year, he would not stop teasing us about it! I really wish I could run!

Robert: Boy are you right! Richard even e-mailed me pictures of the trophy to rub it in! I sure would love to run right over him this year, but I don't see how it can happen without you in the race. We have to have four people to run the relay, and without you we only have three.

Robin: Hey Robert! I just had a great idea! You know that new girl, Rachel, who just moved here from Richmond? I wonder if she could run for me?

Robert: Did she run track in Richmond?

Robin: I don't know, but I saw her running at recess the other day, and she runs pretty fast. It wouldn't hurt to ask!

Robert: She's in my reading class first period. I 'll check with her then!

Robin: Great idea!

The next day in Mrs. Roper's Reading class.

Rachel: Moving is rotten! It's so hard to make new friends when everyone already knows each other. I don't even want to go into the classroom, but I know Mrs. Roper's already seen me. I wish I could just run away. No one is going to talk to me anyway.

Robert: Hi, Rachel! I've been waiting for you. Mrs. Roper is ready to start class, but can I talk to you after class is over? I have a really important question for you.

Rachel: Sure, Robert. OK.

After class.

Rachel: So, Robert, what was it you wanted to ask me?

Robert: We have a really important race this weekend against Rock Hill. Robin usually runs in the relay with us, but she sprained her ankle pretty badly and the doctor said she has to rest this weekend. She can't run in the race.

Rachel: Oh, that's really rough!

Robert: Yeah! But Robin said she saw you running at recess on Friday. She said you were pretty fast. We thought maybe you wouldn't mind running in the race with us.

Rachel: Gosh, Robert, I've never run in a race before. Our school in Richmond didn't have a track team. I don't even really know how a relay works.

Robert: Why don't you come to practice this afternoon and try it out.

Rachel: OK, that sounds good.

Robert: Great! See you then!

That afternoon on the track.

Robin: Hey, Robert. I thought you said you talked to that new girl. She's not here!

Robert: Well, I did talk to her, and she said she'd come. I'm sure she'll try her best to make it.

Rachel: Are you talking about me?

Robin: Hi! Yeah! I'm glad you're here! Robert said you don't know how to race.

Rachel: Right. I'm kind of nervous about this whole thing.

Robert: Oh, don't worry. It'll be really fun! C'mon, girls, let's warm up!

The next day in the cafeteria. The three are sitting together.

Robert: I heard that eating lots of carbohydrates before running is what the professional runners do.

Robin: Super! You love pasta, Robert!

Rachel: Yeah, that's perfect because I brought bread with my lunch today! We should have a great workout after school!

Robert: Well, I'm a little worried about practice today.

Both Girls: Why??

Robert: I've been feeling a little tenderness in my right arm.

Rachel: Well, you don't really use your arm to run, do you?

Robert: No, but it hurts to move it at all and I do move when I run. And that's the arm I use to take the baton. This is a relay you know!

Rachel: What did you do to it to make it hurt?

Robert: I ran into something.

Robin: What did you run into?

Robert: My older brother's fist!

(They all laugh.)

That afternoon on the track.

Robert: Well, let's get started. You want to run a warm-up lap, Rachel?

Rachel: Sure!

Robin: I'll stand here and watch. Ready? GO!!

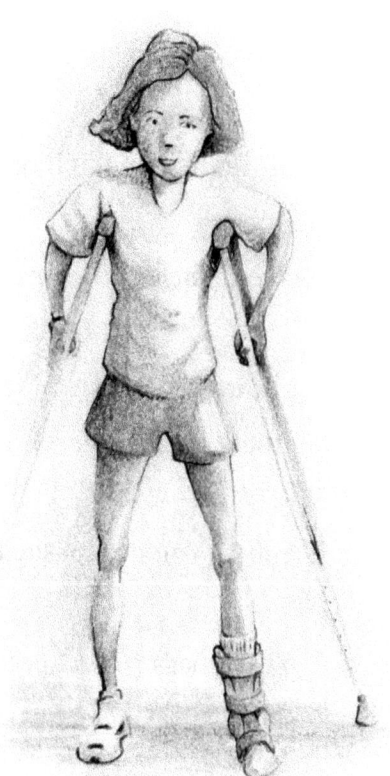

(They begin to run. Robert runs normally for a minute and then grabs his right arm.)

Robert: OUCH!!

Rachel: Robert, are you all right?

Robert: I just wish I could run without my arm hurting!

Rachel: Try running without moving it at all.

(They begin to run again, and this time Robert holds his right arm stiff at his side)

Robin: Robert, you look ridiculous!!!!

Rachel: Yeah! You look like you're part gorilla!!!

(All three stop and laugh hard together.)

Robert: Well, actually it is starting to feel better. Maybe I just need to work out the soreness.

Robin: Well, the race is tomorrow so you'd better work it out fast!

(Rachel looks sad all of a sudden.)

Robert: Hey, Rachel, what's wrong? My arm will be fine by tomorrow.

Rachel: I hope so, but that's not why I'm sad. I'm just really nervous about this race.

Robin: Oh, Rachel, you're going to do great! And I'm really excited, because I just know we're going to run right over Richard!!

Rachel: Who's Richard?

Robert: He's a jerk from Rock Hill who is always bratty about winning races.

Rachel: Oh, he must not have great self-esteem.

Robin: Why would you say that, Rachel?

Rachel: Because, I remember a boy at my old school in Richmond named Roland. He was always rubbing it in when he did better than others at anything. Then, we started being nice to him, and he started being nice back. My mom said he was mean because he was just afraid that no one would like him, so he was mean.

Robert: Man, that sounds backwards. If you're mean, of course no one will like you!

Robin: But I see her point. If you think no one likes you, you feel angry and scared, and that makes you mean, right?

Rachel: Right.

Robert: Well, whatever. I'm not going to worry about Richard. I hope we run the best race ever, and win!!

The next day at the race.

Rachel: Oh, guys, I'm so scared!

Robin: Hey, Rachel, don't worry. You and Robert are the best runners, and we're going to win!!

Robert: Yeah! I'm ready!! My arm feels great, and I ate some macaroni earlier for energy!!

On the track, Robert runs the first leg of the race and hands the baton to Arnie, who then passes it to the third-leg runner Delbert. They are even with the team from Rock Hill when the baton is passed to Rachel and she starts to run. She is even with Richard and then starts to get nervous. She begins to hear the crowd screaming and she slows her pace. As they cross the finish line, Richard is in front of her and wins the race!

The three sit on the grass with the second-place ribbon. Rachel is crying.

Rachel: I'm so sorry!!!

Robin: Hey, Rachel, don't worry about it. I can't remember having more fun at a race, and I didn't even get to run!

Robert: Yeah, it doesn't matter that we lost, because we were able to become friends this week! That's really what makes a team work!!

Rachel: But remember? You both wanted to beat Richard from Rock Hill!

Robert: I think we did beat him.

Both girls: What?

Robert: Look over there. His team won't even talk to him because he's hoarding the first place ribbons and not sharing them. The three of us are more of a team than they are. That makes us the real winners!

Rachel Runs the Race

New Vocabulary:
relay race
track
carbohydrates
professional
nervous
hording

Comprehension Questions:

1. What was the problem at the beginning of the play? What solution did Robin suggest?

2. Why did Robert and Robin want to beat Rock Hill in the Relay Race?

3. How did Rachel feel about starting at a new school?

4. What are some of the things the team did to get ready for the race?

5. What did Rachel suggest might be the reason behind Richard's bad attitude?

6. Why did Robert say their team was the real winner?

7. Tell about a time when you were new. Did you feel like Rachel felt?

8. What does it mean to be part of a team? What kind of responsibilities do you share?

9. What would you say to Richard if he were to ask you why no one liked him?

10. What does it mean to be a "good sport"?

Rachel Runs the Race

Teacher's Guide

Comprehension Questions:

1. What was the problem at the beginning of the play? What solution did Robin suggest?
   Robin couldn't run in the relay race because she sprained her ankle. She suggested asking Rachel to run in the race in her place.

2. Why did Robert and Robin want to beat Rock Hill in the Relay Race?
   Rock Hill won last year and teased them about it.

3. How did Rachel feel about starting at a new school?
   She was very nervous and scared.

4. What are some of the things the team did to get ready for the race?
   Practiced and ate good foods.

5. What did Rachel suggest might be the reason behind Richard's bad attitude?
   He had really low self-esteem.

6. Why did Robert say their team was the real winner?
   They learned how to work as a team.

7. Tell about a time when you were new. Did you feel like Rachel felt?
   Answers will vary.

8. What does it mean to be part of a team? What kind of responsibilities do you share?
   Answers will vary.

9. What would you say to Richard if he were to ask you why no one liked him?
   Answers will vary.

10. What does it mean to be a "good sport"?
    Answers will vary.

Language Extensions:
- Social language: starting a new school, making new friends, dealing with emotions.

Rachel Runs the Race

Activity: Rachel had to learn to meet new friends when she moved to a new school. Sometimes it's hard to know what to say when you meet new people. Richard has trouble making friends, too, because he chooses to behave in a way that is not very likeable. Think about the different situations below. Find a partner and role-play what you would say in these situations. Don't forget to use your good speech skills!

Situation 1: You see a new student who has just started at your school. Introduce yourself and invite them to do something you enjoy doing.

Situation 2: Someone spills their tray of food in the cafeteria. Go and offer to help. What can you say to help the person feel less embarrassed?

Situation 3: You are chosen to be the team captain in P.E. Talk with your friend about who you will choose for your team, and how you can make sure you don't hurt anyone's feelings.

Situation 4: Your friend told you a secret and you told it to someone else. Your friend is very upset. Talk to your friend. What can you say to try to make things better?

Situation 5: Another boy in the school said something that hurt your feelings. Tell him how it made you feel.

Situation 6: You are playing a game with a friend. Your friend isn't following the rules correctly. Talk to your friend about how you think the game is supposed to be played.

Situation 7: Your friend's dog just died. She comes to sit with you at lunch. What will you say to your friend?

Rachel Runs the Race

WORD LIST

INITIAL	INTERNAL and FINAL	BLENDS
Robert	doctor	pretty
Robin	four	trophy
Rachel	three	great
run	other	track
relay	hurt	sprained
rest	her	practice
right	hard	try
Rock Hill	already	professionals
runner	everyone	brought
Richard	classroom	bread
rub	important	bratty
Richmond	before	angry
recess	afternoon	crowd
reading	nervous	screaming
rotten	warm	cross
Mrs. Roper's	cafeteria	grass
ready	together	friends
rough	carbohydrates	
really	super	
ran	perfect	
ridiculous	worried	
Rodney	tenderness	
rubbing	arm	
ribbon	hurt	
	older	
	brother	
	started	
	sure	
	gorilla	
	soreness	
	tomorrow	
	work	
	jerk	
	better	
	others	
	scared	
	macaroni	
	energy	
	hoarding	
	winners	

The Contest

The Contest

Characters:

Narrator
Rattlesnake
Monitor Lizard
Scorpion

Narrator: A monitor lizard and a rattlesnake were lying in the sun one afternoon. They had known each other for a long time and were always competing in one way or another. Last Thursday, the lizard bet the rattlesnake that he could crawl faster than the rattlesnake could slither. The Friday before that, they battled over who was the better dancer. Every week they warred with each other over some silly skill, and this week was no different.

Rattlesnake: Hey Lizard! I believe it's time for you to say that I am the better reptile! So far, the score is 7-6 in my favor. I'll always come in first!

Lizard: No way, Rattler! I'm just coming into my prime! You set the goal and I'll reach it, no problem! So far, I've just been warming up!

Rattlesnake: Is that so? Well then, let's have one final grand contest and settle this once and for all. The winner of this contest will be named the Lord of the Reptiles and King of the Desert! Are you up for it?

Lizard: You just be ready to serve my every need, Rattler! As Lord of the Reptiles I'll need servants like you.

Rattlesnake: You talk big now, but I wonder what you'll be saying when I claim first prize.

Lizard: Well, then let's stop this war of words and get to the more important matter of setting the tasks for our contest.

Rattlesnake: Of course, Lizard! Here's what we'll do. We'll have four tasks. You will determine two and I will determine two. Whoever completes the most tasks first, wins.

Lizard: That sounds reasonable, Rattler, but what will we do in the case of a tie?

Rattlesnake: Hmm. I'm not sure.

Lizard: I know! We'll let Scorpion decide a final test if we can't resolve the dispute.

Rattlesnake: Agreed! Scorpion will respect the rules of the contest! He'll determine the winner.

Lizard: Then we'll meet tomorrow on the riverbank at three o'clock. Let the best reptile win!

Narrator: That night, Lizard and Rattlesnake lay awake in their burrows trying to think of the perfect tasks for their competition. Lizard tried to think of tasks where he could use his arms and legs, since the snake had neither. The rattlesnake also tried to think of tasks where his strengths would help him defeat the lizard. Before they knew it, the sun was rising over the rocks, and it was almost time for the contest.

Scorpion: Okay, Lizard! Time to rise and shine! The morning is starting without us!

Lizard: I have to think of tasks that I can do well, but that Rattler can't. I'm much better at working with my hands. Ha ha! I know! We'll see how good Rattler is at throwing darts! Why, he won't even be able to hold them!

Scorpion: C'mon, Rattlesnake. Time for you to rise and shine, too! The moment has arrived for your Reptilathon!

Rattler: Now let's see. What is something I can do that Lizard can't? I am so good at slithering! Lizard can't get under anything! Let's see how good Lizard is at crawling under barbed wire! I bet he'll hit it every time!

Lizard: Hello there, Rattler! Are you ready for our first task?

Rattler: I'm always ready, Lizard. Since you are the loser so far, I'll let you chose our first task. I hope you're ready to lose!

Lizard: Oh, no. This time we will work on something much more challenging than our last skirmish. Are you up for a game of darts? Scorpion has nailed my dartboard to that cactus over there. Let's see who can get the best score out of three darts.

Scorpion: OK, boys. Take your shots. Best of three wins!

Narrator: Rattler looked a bit worried as he watched lizard throw all three darts close to the center of the target. When his turn came, he tried to balance the darts on his head and hurl them at the target by whacking them with his rattle. This didn't work well at all, and Rattler didn't get a single dart to stick in the target.

Lizard: Well, I guess we know who the better dart-thrower is in the reptile world. I guess rattlesnakes don't make good dart-throwers. I told you lizards are the better reptiles. Only lizards can throw darts!

Scorpion: Children know so little. Can't they see what is really important? It's certainly not throwing darts!

Rattlesnake: What good is throwing darts anyway? I have never had need to throw a dart! What a silly sport! My task is much more difficult and much more important!

Narrator: Rattlesnake led Lizard over to where two trees had fallen. Rattlesnake had asked Scorpion to stretch barbed wire between the trees so that it was only a few inches off the ground.

Rattlesnake: Now, Lizard, let's see who is the best reptile. This task is a race, but not just any race! The winner is the reptile who crawls or slithers the fastest under this sharp barbed wire without a scratch. We're ready when you are, Scorpion.

Scorpion: Ready? On your mark…get set….GO! Or slide, or crawl, or whatever you're supposed to be learning from this race.

Narrator: Lizard struggled to crawl under the barbed wire, but as he was made to crawl on his legs, he was not as close to the ground as the rattlesnake. The rattlesnake slithered quickly and gracefully beneath the wire and made it to the other side with no trouble at all.

Rattlesnake: Oh, Lizard, are you not able to get under the wire? Hmmm, that's too bad. I suppose rattlesnakes are the greatest reptiles then. Moving quickly and getting in and around dangerous areas would be an important skill for the Lord of the Reptiles. Don't you agree, Scorpion?

Scorpion: Oh, well, not being a reptile myself, I'm afraid I wouldn't know the exact use of barbed-wire crawling in the desert.

Lizard: Just because I don't crawl on my belly doesn't mean I can't get in and around dangerous areas! That task was unfair!

Rattlesnake: No more unfair than throwing darts! This contest is about whose strengths are more important when tackling danger in the desert! The rattlesnake is the strongest reptile!

Scorpion: Children, children. Simmer down.

Lizard: Monitor lizards are much stronger than rattlesnakes! I will prove that in our next task. Are you ready?

Rattlesnake: Bring it on!

Scorpion: Oh, I've already brought it on and built it for you. Don't worry.

Lizard: You see those rocks piled high over there? The first reptile to climb to the top of those rocks will win this task. We're ready, Scorpion.

Scorpion: Ready? On your mark…get set…GO!! And please mind the first few rocks. I had trouble getting them to rest perfectly on each other.

Narrator: The monitor lizard did not move quite as quickly as the rattlesnake, but once they reached the pile of rocks the lizard was able to climb much more easily than the snake. The rattlesnake was not able to climb from one rock to another without a flat surface to slither on. The lizard, however, was able to grasp footholds in the rock, and quickly scrambled to the top.

Lizard: Aha! Now you see how strong a lizard can be! And clearly crawling atop rocks is a very important skill for the King of the Desert!

Narrator: They continued to war with each other, hurling angry taunts, and arguing about whose strengths were more important in the desert.

Rattlesnake: We still have another task to complete, Lizard! When you are ready, I will inform you of what it will be.

Lizard: I am always ready for you, Rattler!

Rattlesnake: Well then, in this event, we'll see who can make the four basic knots: a square knot, a half hitch, a double half hitch, and a simple over hand knot. Get ready…

Lizard: Wait!! What am I supposed to make these knots with?

Rattlesnake: Well, that's part of the test isn't it? Ready…go!

Lizard: Scorpion! Help me!

Scorpion: As I am not a reptile, I really can't get involved, Lizard. Sorry.

Narrator: Lizard grumbled and growled as he scrounged around looking for something he could use to tie a knot. Before he found anything, Rattlesnake had twisted his frame so that all four knots were made perfectly along his long body.

Lizard: Fine! You win that battle, but that still makes the score…what, Scorpion?

Scorpion: You are two against two at this moment.

Lizard: Great. Scorpion will decide the Lord of the Reptiles. I know that he will agree that my strengths are much more important than yours.

Rattlesnake: We'll see. He's been watching our contest this whole time. He'll tell us who deserves to be Lord of the Reptiles and King of the Desert.

Scorpion: Oh, brother. I'm the tie-breaker?

Narrator: And so the rattlesnake and the lizard turned to Scorpion and demanded he name a winner. Scorpion merely sat there looking at the two of them. Finally, he took a deep breath and said:

Scorpion: I can't make this decision until I have my lucky horseshoe returned. The vulture has stolen it again and placed it atop the tallest cactus in the desert. Find my horseshoe, and I'll give you my answer.

Lizard: But where is the tallest cactus in the desert?

Rattlesnake: I think I know. I'm able to travel all over this desert. I have seen every inch, and I know exactly which cactus Scorpion means!

Lizard: Well then, let's hurry so we can have this matter settled!

Rattlesnake: Certainly!

Scorpion: I pray for a safe return for you both.

Narrator: Lizard and Rattlesnake crossed the desert looking for the tallest cactus, in which they knew they would find Scorpion's horseshoe. When they found the cactus, they realized that it was so thickly covered with needles, that there was no way either of them would be able to climb it.

Lizard: How are we going to get to the top? Those needles would cut us to shreds if either of us were to try to climb it!

Rattlesnake: I can stretch high enough to reach it, but then I wouldn't be able to wrap around it without getting close to those needles!

Lizard: Well, I could grab it, but I can't get high enough to reach it!

Rattlesnake: Here, I know! You stand on my head and I'll lift you up to reach it.

Lizard: Great idea!

Narrator: Lizard scurried up on Rattlesnake's head and was raised up until he was even with the top of the cactus. Lizard quickly reached out and grabbed the horseshoe.

Lizard: I got it! Let's get this back to Scorpion!

Narrator: The two reptiles rushed the crest back to Scorpion, anxious for him to finally make the decision on whose strengths were worthy of the title Lord of the Reptiles.

Rattlesnake: Scorpion! We found your horseshoe! Now tell us your decision!

Scorpion: The winner is the one who was able to get my lucky horseshoe.

Rattlesnake: Oh, well, I had no way to grab it, so Lizard, I guess you're actually the one who deserves the prize.

Lizard: Oh, no. There was no way for me to reach it without your lifting me. So, Rattler, you're the rightful winner.

Scorpion: It sounds as though you have learned the most important rule of the desert! You have each been given certain strengths; strengths that are needed to survive in the rough terrain. But the most important strength that you have is each other. Learn to work together and any task can be overcome!

The Contest

New Vocabulary:

monitor lizard
skirmish
barbed wire
taunt
terrain

burrows
strengths
slither
resolve
scrounged
vulture

Comprehension Questions:

1. Compare and contrast the monitor lizard and the rattlesnake. In what ways are they the same? In what ways are they different?

2. What was the competition about? What type of tasks did Lizard and Rattlesnake try to think of?

3. What made Scorpion a good choice to decide the winner in the case of a tie?

4. What was the first task in the contest? In what ways was this task unfair?

5. Why did the lizard have a hard time with the second task?

6. What made the third task easier for the lizard?

7. How did Rattlesnake make the last task more difficult for Lizard?

8. What did Scorpion ask the rattlesnake and lizard to do in order to determine the winner of the contest?

9. What lesson did the rattlesnake and lizard learn in the end?

10. What are some of your strengths? How do your strengths help you in your tasks throughout the day?

The Contest

Teacher's Guide

Comprehension Questions:

1. Compare and contrast the monitor lizard and the rattlesnake. In what ways are they the same? In what ways are they different?
   See page 87

2. What was the competition about? What type of tasks did Lizard and Rattlesnake try to think of?
   They were battling over who was the greatest reptile. Lizard and Rattlesnake tried to think of tasks that they would be better suited for.

3. What made Scorpion a good choice to decide the winner in the case of a tie?
   He would respect the rules of the contest. He isn't a reptile.

4. What was the first task in the contest? In what ways was this task unfair?
   Darts. This was unfair because the rattlesnake doesn't have any hands to hold the darts.

5. Why did the lizard have a hard time with the second task?
   His legs made it difficult for him to get low to the ground.

6. What made the third task easier for the lizard?
   He could crawl up on the rocks with his legs.

7. How did Rattlesnake make the last task more difficult for Lizard?
   He didn't give Lizard a rope.

8. What did Scorpion ask the rattlesnake and lizard to do in order to determine the winner of the contest?
   Find his lucky horseshoe.

9. What lesson did the rattlesnake and lizard learn in the end?
   They each have different strengths and weaknesses, but if they worked together, they could complete a task that neither could finish alone.

10. What are some of your strengths? How do your strengths help you in your tasks throughout the day?
    Answers will vary

Language Extensions:
- Compare and contrast
- Describing

85

The Contest

Compare and Contrast: Use the graphic organizer below to outline ways in which the rattlesnake and lizard are alike and ways they are different.

The Contest

Activity: Use the graphic organizer below to outline ways in which the rattlesnake and lizard are alike and ways they are different.

TTLESNAKE
No arms or legs
Good at slithering
Low to the ground
Long body

Both are reptiles
Both can get in and around small places

LIZARD
Has legs
Can grasp with hands

The Contest

WORD LIST

INITIAL	INTERNAL and FINAL	BLENDS
rattlesnake	lizard	Friday
reach	scorpion	crawl
reptiles	afternoon	prize
resolve	slither	strengths
respect	desert	throw
riverbank	servants	scratch
rocks	war	ground
Rattler	determine	trouble
rest	burrows	agree
ready	arms	stronger
raised	first	grasp
rushed	score	scrambled
rule	hurl	grumbled
rough	target	growled
	sport	scrounged
	barbed	frame
	wire	travel
	sharp	pray
	learning	crossed
	dangerous	shreds
	unfair	stretch
	surface	wrap
	important	grab
	square	
	vulture	
	terrain	

www.ingramcontent.com/pod-product-compliance
Lightning Source LLC
Chambersburg PA
CBHW080447110426
42743CB00016B/3307